HER PURSE SMELLED LIKE JUICY FRUIT

This Book is dedicated to my wife, my daughters, my grandchildren, and most of all my mother
Louise Wilson.

Thank you:
Kresge Arts in Detroit, The Corporation of Yaddo, ArtServe of Michigan,
Beverly McIver, Judy Sledge, Nancy Mitchnick, Chris Schneider/Hatch,
Mildred Davis, Steven Wilson, Kenneth Wilson, Carlespie McKinney,
and the good people of Parkhurst Place.

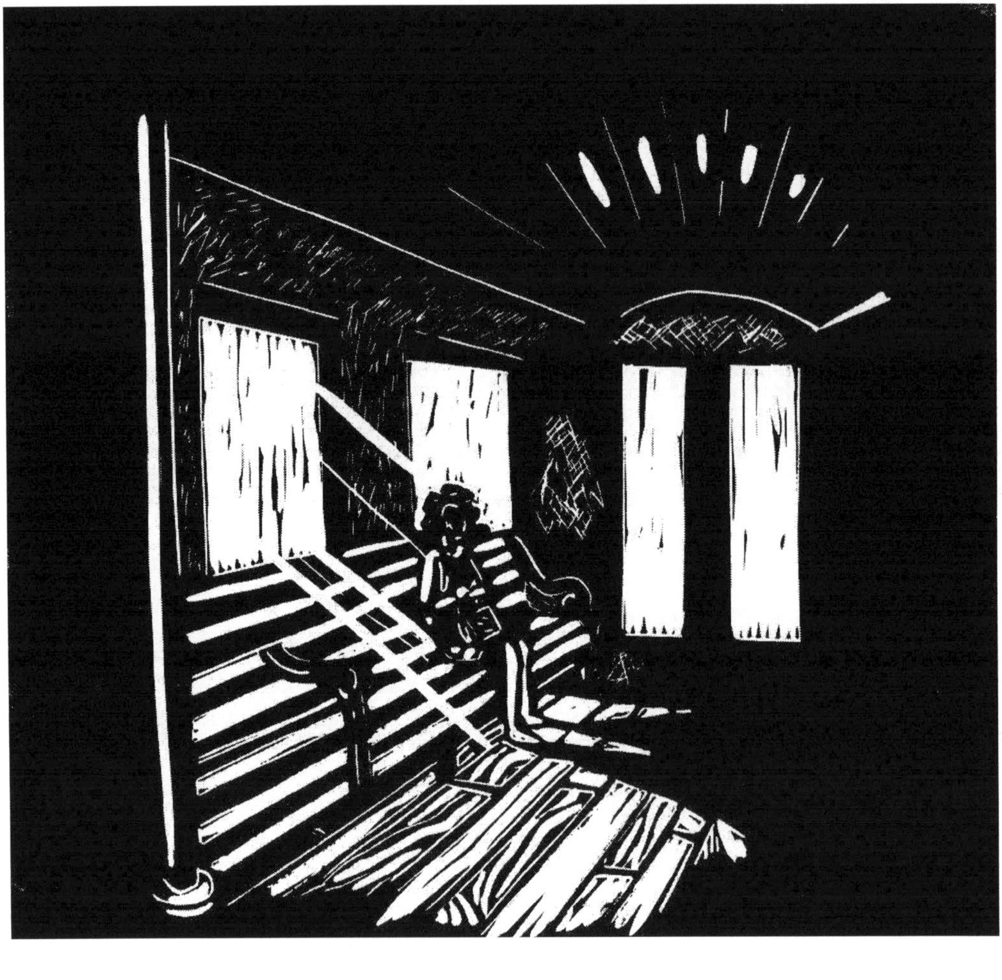

HER PURSE SMELLED LIKE JUICY FRUIT

Linocut Art By Carl Wilson

With a personal foreword by
Mariuca Rofick

THE LOFT HOUSE PRESS
HAMTRAMCK

THE LOFT HOUSE PRESS

CARL WILSON

Library of Congress Cataloging-In-Publication Data

ISBN 978-0-578-45890-8

Made In the United States

Foreword

I have had the pleasure of seeing Carl's prints from the beginning, in 2008. His first print, *Aisha from Linwood*, was interesting and drew me into the medium in general. His second print, *Waiting for My Change to Come* completely blew me away! He had somehow managed to carve a deeply poignant-bordering-on-spiritual element into this print. I commandeered a copy for my own collection (which I continue to zealously guard) and subsequently eagerly awaited each new print. I was not disappointed, as he produced one after another over the next few years, continuing to instill a similar depth of emotion as he carved scenes from his life and of the world around him.

By early 2013 Carl had created a series of prints called Parkhurst Papers, which was exhibited at The Detroit Repertory Theatre. A selection of prints from that series was submitted to the Kresge Foundation and Carl was chosen to receive a 2013 Kresge Fellowship in the visual arts. The fellowship allowed Carl to purchase a press (no more printing by hand!) and also helped position him to experience the residency at Yaddo where he printed the majority of prints in this series about his mom.

I regret that I never got to meet my mother-in-law. I have learned so much about her through Carl and his siblings and have grown quite fond of her. I can say from firsthand experience that her children are salt of the earth, smart, and funny as hell. I couldn't be happier or more proud that Carl chose to memorialize her life in the way he knows best—through printmaking.

Mariuca Rofick

About My Mother

This isn't a biography of Louise Wilson as such. It's impossible to write anything even remotely close to a complete biography about her. Hopefully you will read these few words and catch enough of an air about her to appreciate the artwork contained in these pages. Please read between the lines.

Louise Josephine Agnew was born in Asheville, North Carolina. I only recently found out the year she was born. She kept that fact hidden from me her entire life. It wasn't for a lack of trying that I didn't know. I asked her many times and the answer was always the same. She would look around for effect, lower her voice, and very quietly ask, "Can you keep a secret?" Eagerly I would shake my silly head yes. "I can too," was her reply. A month before the publication of this book I found out the year of her birth. She would be proud to know I too can keep a secret.

She grew up in a large family of either ten or eleven. Her father Russell Agnew was a working man who did something—I was never privy to what—for a living. He made nine dollars a week. She loved him dearly.

I met her mother once. She came to Detroit from North Carolina for a visit and stayed with us for about a week. She said very little to me that I can recall, but one comment stayed with me: she said I had pretty legs, almost like a girl's.

But I digress. Somewhere along the line Ma came to Detroit, and worked at several menial labor jobs. She once told a story about being in Michigan's Upper Peninsula and having little white children follow her down the street asking where was her tail. There also was a story about waitressing at White Tower Hamburgers and all the "colored" girls being let go during the recession, because “good white women” needed the work. She never said a bad word about persecutors. I remember she somehow managed to relate these stories and emit an air of dignity. She taught us to combat ignorance with excellence.

While in Detroit she met my father, William Wilson, and they had my siblings and me. She and my father argued bitterly, as far back as I can remember.

When she died, my father cried in anguish. He never got over her loss.

She was an excellent grandmother to all of her grandchildren and a woman of uncommon strength. She buried one grandchild, my sister’s son. Although I knew her heart was broken she would not allow herself to cry in front of us. I believe she felt she had to be the strong one for all of us.

I don’t recall a tender touch, or warm embrace. I don’t mourn that because I believe she felt life would be too hard for a sensitive, girl-legged fellow like me and I needed to get tough as soon as possible and stay tough.

I have no doubt she loved me more than she loved herself.

She was the picture of strength and grace. I will love her forever,

This book of art is for her.

CW

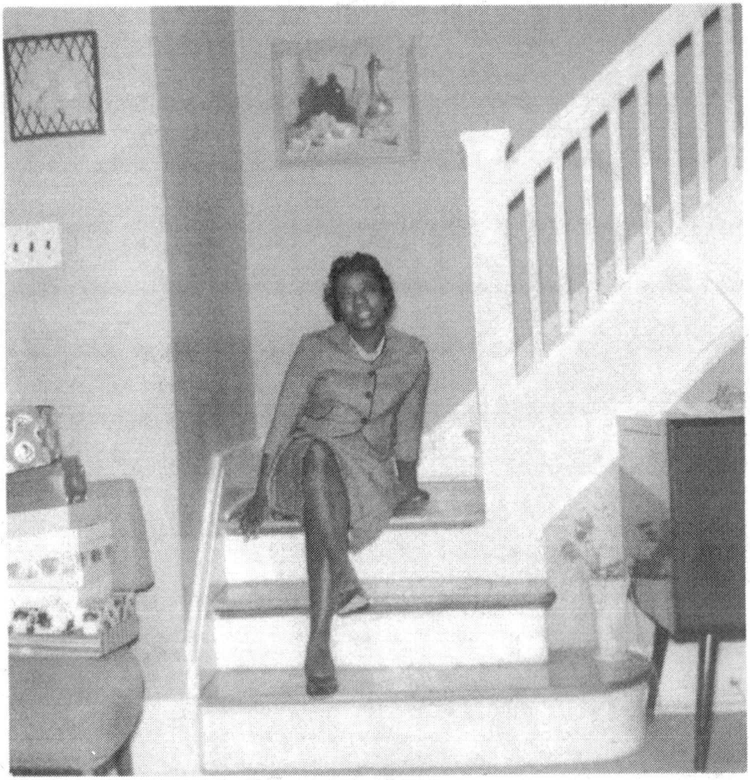

the prints

Goethe

linocut, 9x12

When I was five years old I formulated an image of my mother. She was tough and aloof and I loved her anyway. That image was cast in stone when we lived in a mouse-infested apartment on Goethe Street on Detroit's lower east side. She washed our clothes in the rodent overrun basement and never let me go down there with her no matter how much I begged. All I ever saw was her disappearing and returning from a dark hole.

I never saw my mother cry. I was very surprised years later when she told me she cried every day we lived there. She was afraid of mice. I had no idea.

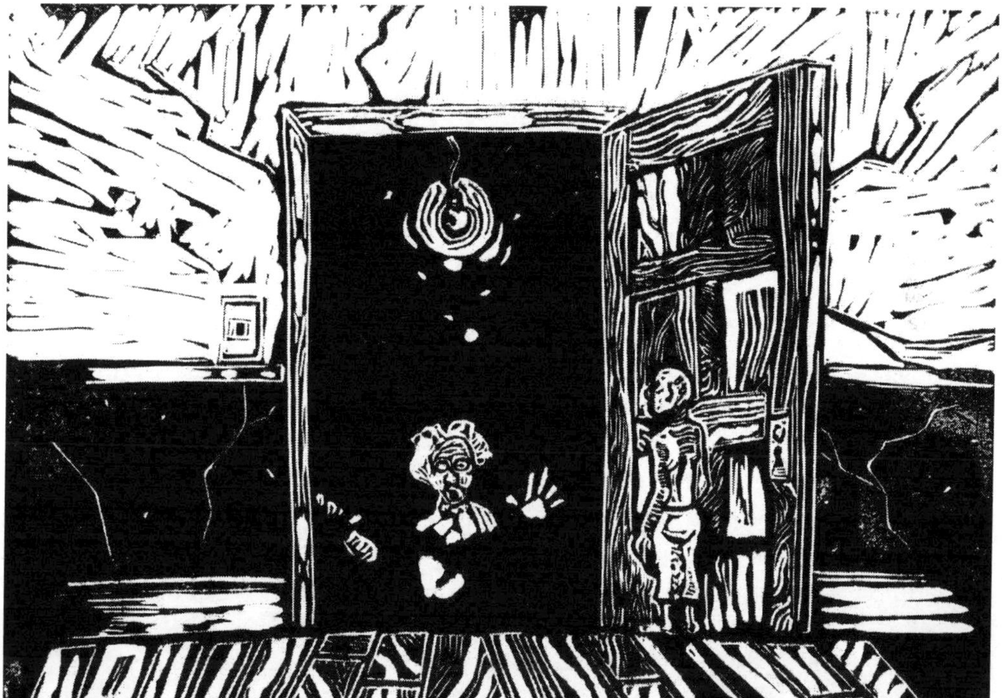

Chicken Delight

linocut, 8x10

A family friend, Mr. Sam, got a new Cadillac. He drove it to our house and took our family out for a meal. This had NEVER happened before. I was excited beyond belief. We didn't own a car at the time and here I was riding in the back seat of a Cadillac *and* going out to eat! My father had a characteristically dour look plastered on his face the entire ride. My mother sat quietly tight-lipped holding her ever-present purse. We pulled into the parking lot of Chicken Delight. What was this strangely delightful aromatic place? Hubba Bubba! Mr. Sam is giving us chicken drumsticks! Woo-Hoo! They're drizzled with honey!

I ruined my mother's day dancing around the parking lot like a clown on a string in complete and utter bliss. "Oh you idiots. Please stop, you're embarrassing me."

No chicken has tasted as good since.

This print was carved at Yaddo in Saratoga Springs. I washed it with what I thought was a safe solvent. It wasn't. The synthetic linoleum I use melted before I could get the desired result in the printing process.

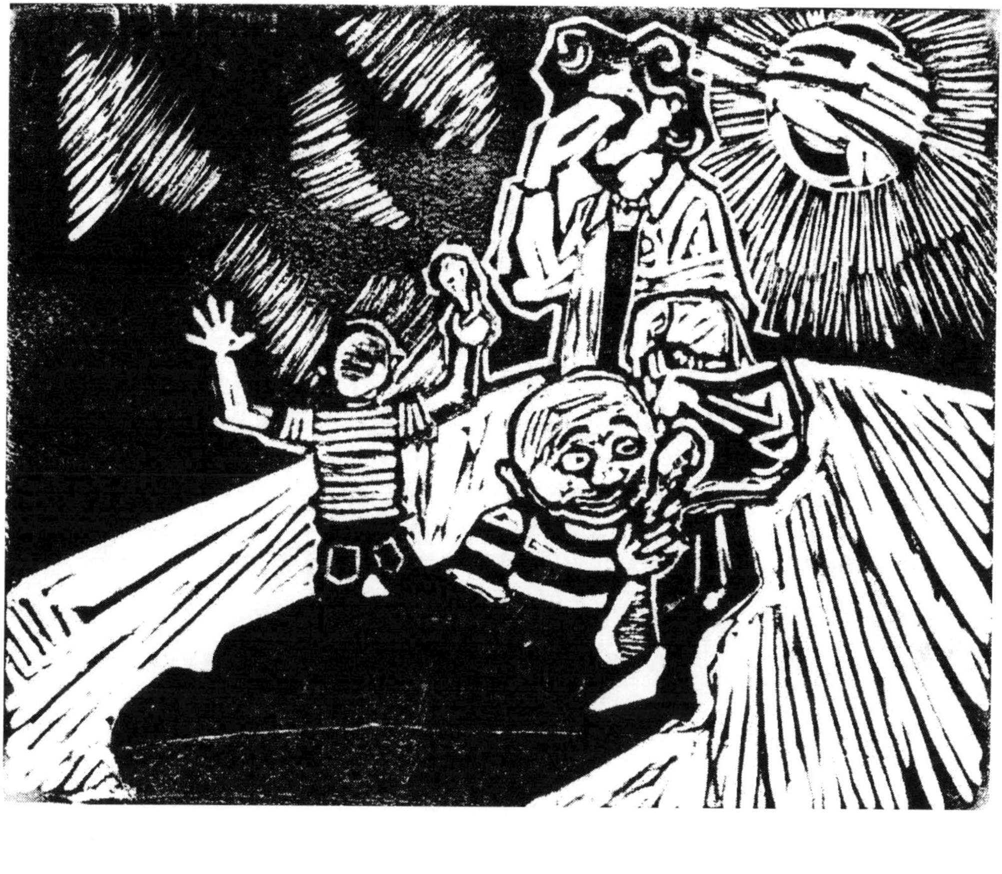

Getting To The Bottom Of It

linocut, 12x18

This is one of the first stories I considered telling in this project. One of my mother's sisters was murdered in New York City and Mom went there to get to the bottom of things. I have no idea how that worked out because she never told me. I don't even remember who told me this story. Someone may have gone with her. Again, I don't know whom. You will notice her face is not clearly seen in many of these prints. That's because I realize how little I know about her. She kept herself hidden from me. I did eventually tackle a portrait of her as part of the project because there is a photo of her in her younger days that is etched in my memory. This project has reaffirmed how dysfunctional my upbringing was. Bad for me. Good for my art.

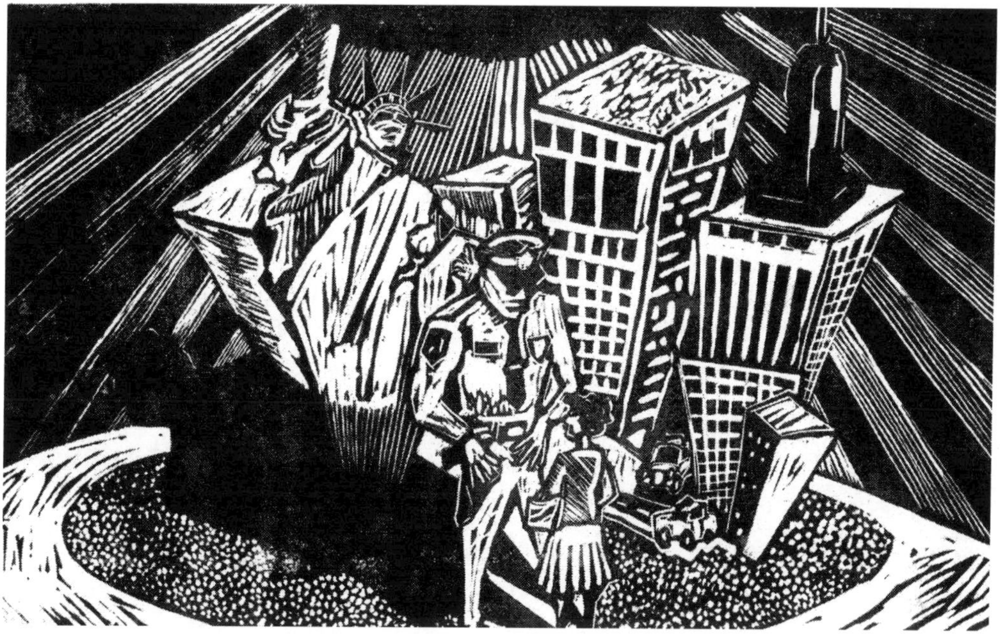

Asheville

linocut, 9x12

I believe my mother had eight siblings. Every year at Christmastime she told me all she and her brothers and sisters got as presents was an apple or orange and a pair of socks. I thought it was just another *I want to be cheap and not buy you anything* story so I paid it little attention. As a child it didn’t occur to me a Black family of eleven in the 1920s couldn't do much better than that. Her family was probably much better off than many in the community. In her honor I will only give my children and grandchildren fruit and socks from now on.

That is me being cheap.

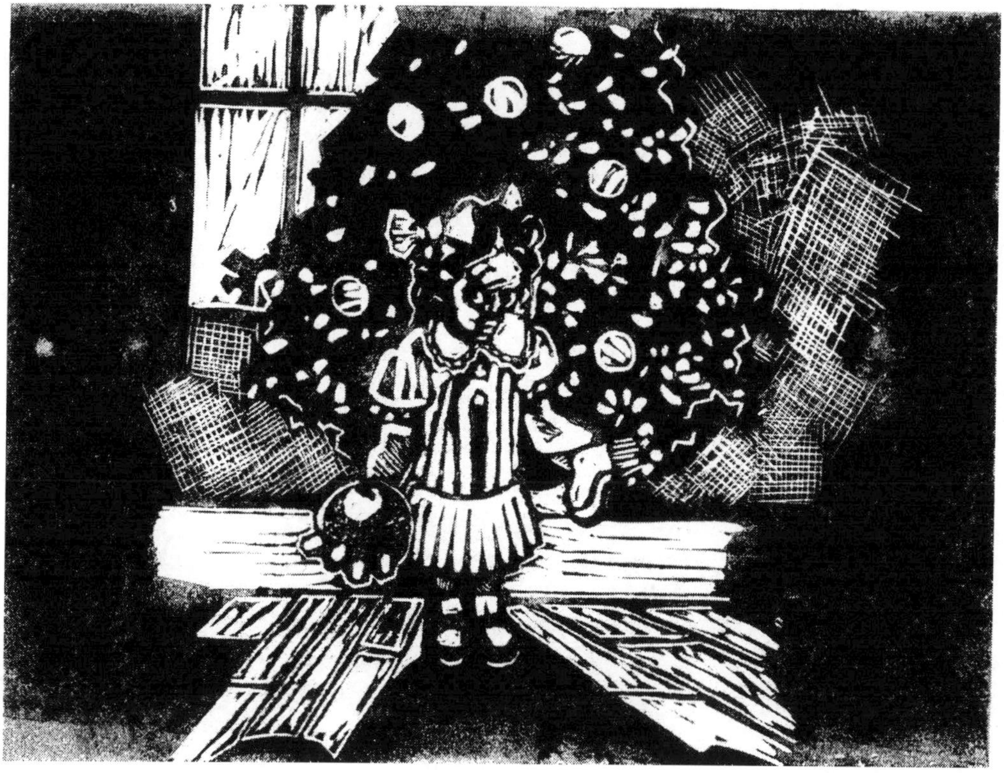

St. Louise Chains
The Dragon King Of Pain

linocut, 9x12

My father was a handsome, charming, and debonair man. A talented, but frustrated artist in his own right, that handsome, debonair fellow went far away one day. A terrifying brute, a diagnosed paranoid schizophrenic, replaced him. He was hearing voices and seeing things, arguing simultaneously with God and The Devil.

My mother handled my father's mental illness the same way she handled everything—privately and without excess emotion. Mom did what she could. It wasn't nearly enough, but she had nothing to work with. She kept us from getting seriously physically hurt and I guess that was the most important thing.

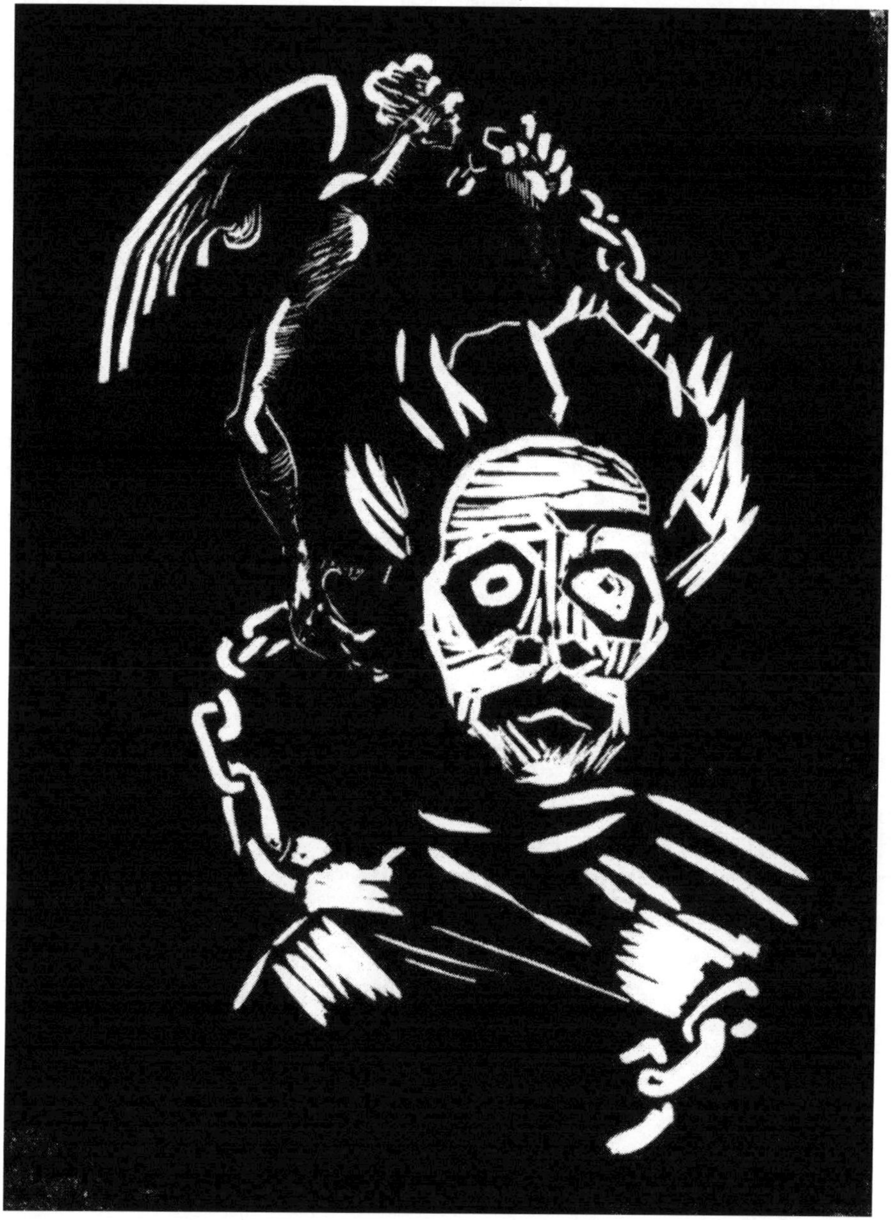

Up On A Tightrope

linocut, 8x10

This portrait of my mother is based on the photograph at the beginning of this book. It must have been taken in 1959 or 1960. She was sitting on the staircase of our rat's nest apartment on Goethe Street in Detroit. The picture was totally out of character for her. She is dressed up in a suit with her legs crossed like she hasn't a care in the world.

Years later I found out she loved Leon Russell's song *Tightrope*. Not surprising because her taste in music ran from Hank Williams to Chopin. The song uses circus imagery as a metaphor for Russell's complicated life. My mother was a bit of a circus performer and tightrope walker as well. I would never figure her out, but I kept getting little glimpses of her if I looked around closely enough. In this print she wears a mask obscuring her face because she purposely kept me from ever really knowing her.

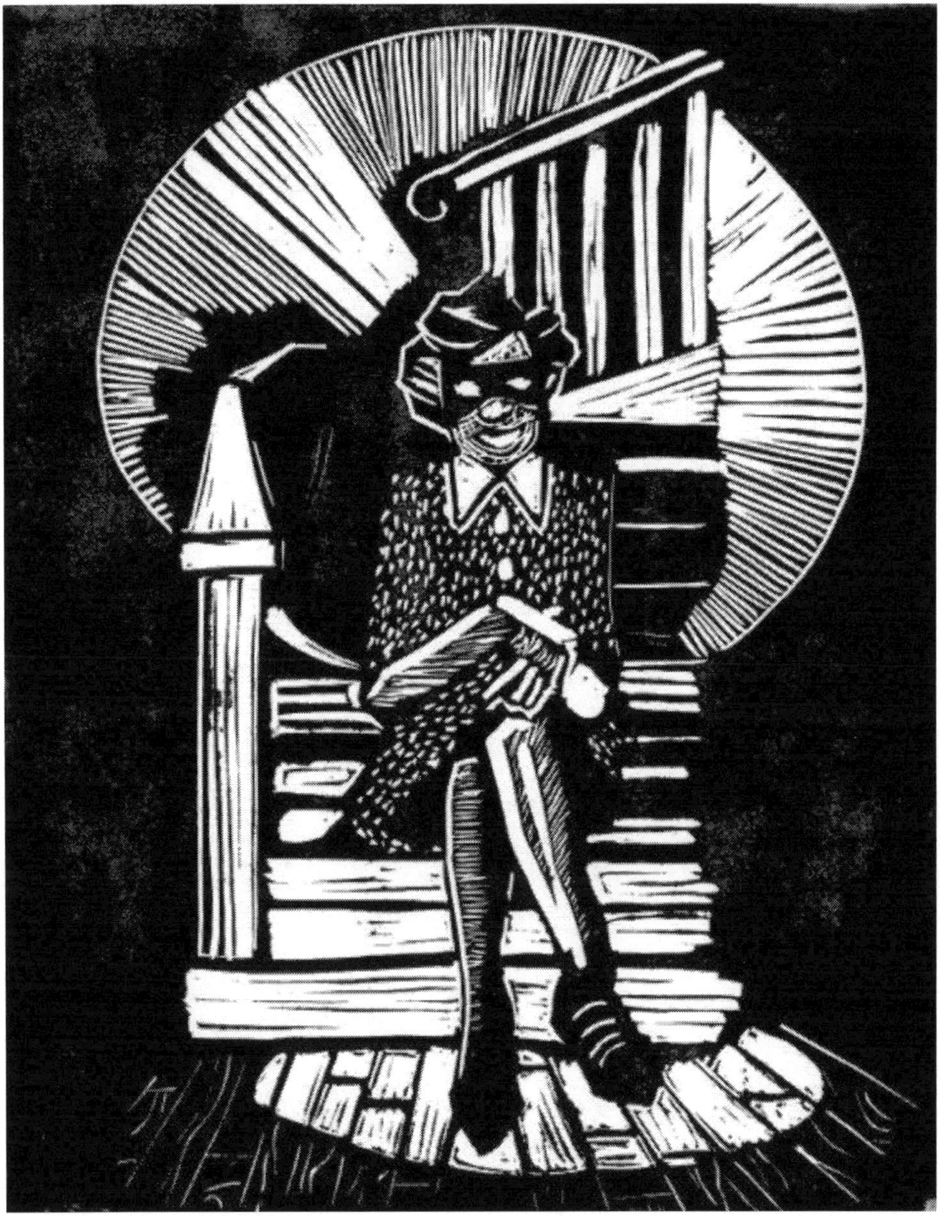

Her Purse Smelled Like Juicy Fruit

linocut, 12x12

This print captures what I wanted to say about Ma. It is purely speculative. She's on a train. She could be headed to Detroit. She could be headed to the bottom of things in New York investigating murders and whatnot. I know so little about her. She sits alone, backlit by intense light that obscures the truth about her appearance and reality. The one thing I know for sure is she ALWAYS carried a purse and it always smelled like Juicy Fruit gum. It was one of the most pure pleasures I had, to sneak and smell her open purse. Even now, whenever I catch that scent I think of her.

I see her now as complete within herself. It was her right. I'm at peace with that.

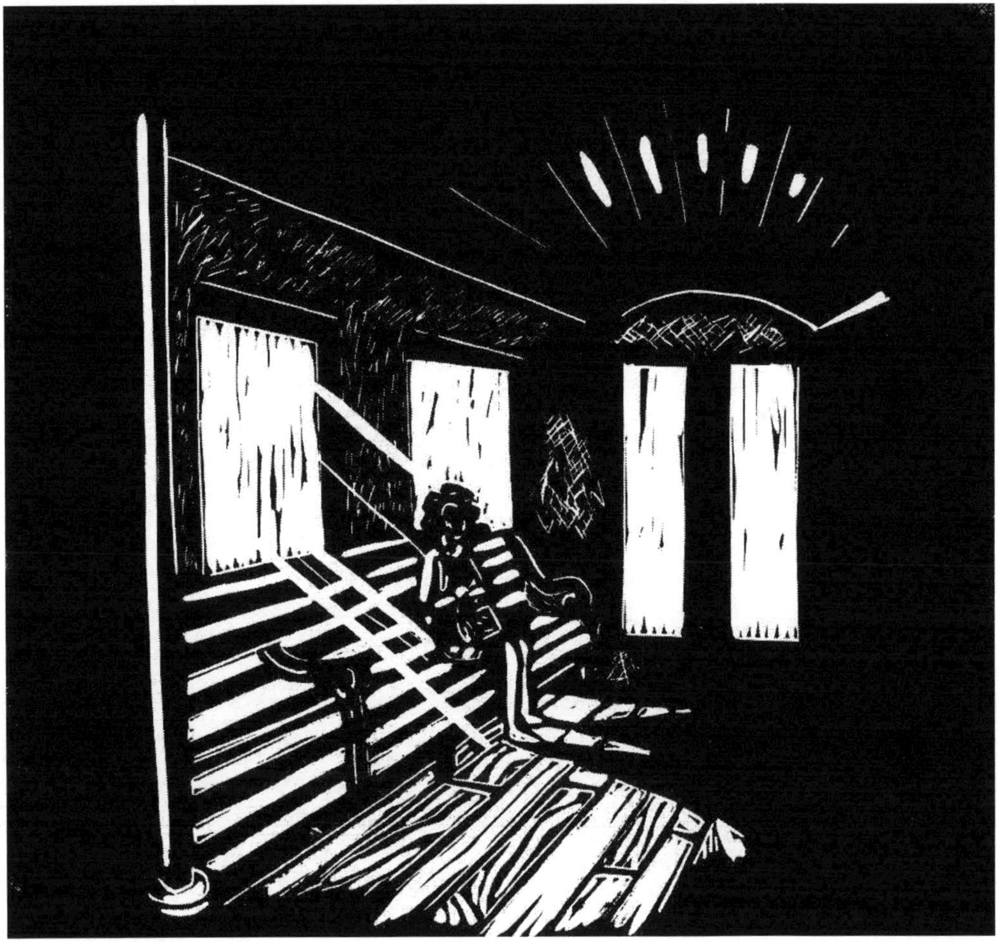

Keep It Moving

linocut, 12x12

After my dad's breakdown he was incapable of working. In fact he never held another job in his life. To take care of all of us, including Dad, my mom got a job at Marxhausen Elementary School, across the street from our house. She was a lunch lady. I don't think I was embarrassed by it. I think my youngest brother Kenneth may have been teased about it after I departed for junior high. Mom seemed to like it. Later she got a promotion of sorts and became a teacher's aid. I lied and told people she was a teacher. I am sorry I was shallow like that, but in my defense she always seemed like a teacher to me.

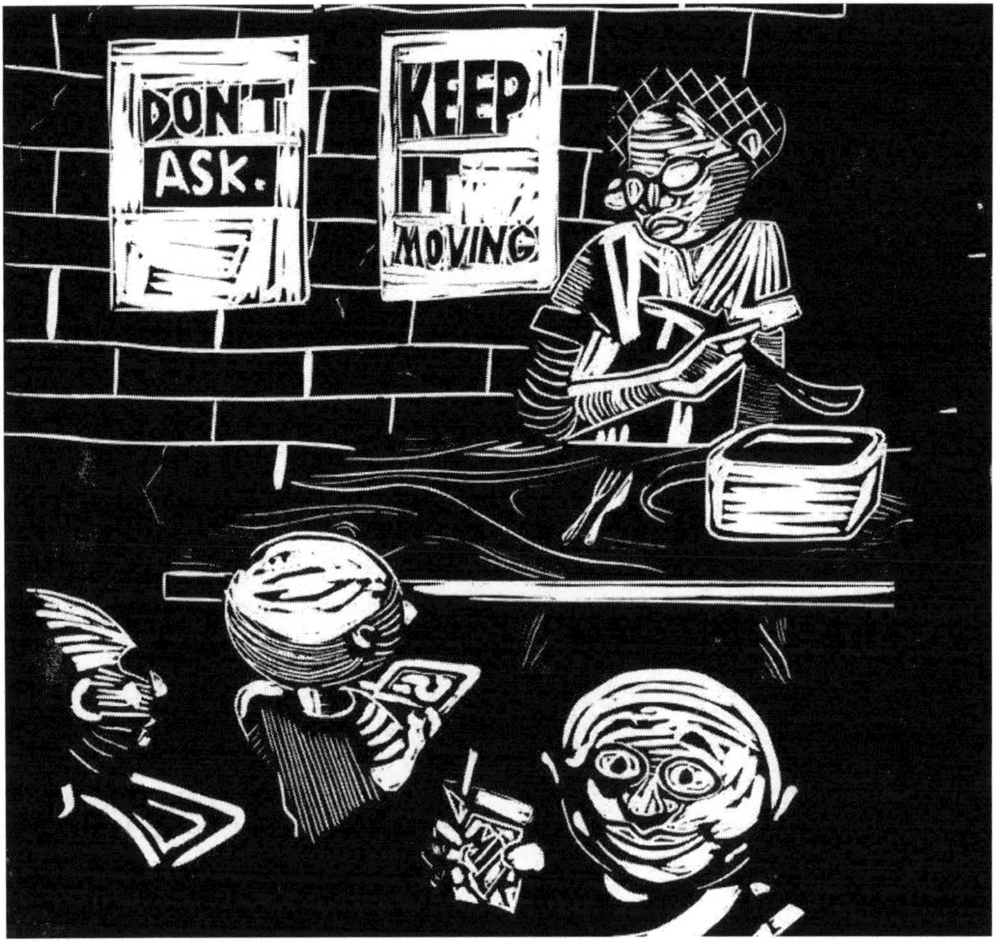
DON'T
ASK.
KEEP
IT
MOVING

Mom Always Liked You Best

linocut, 9x12

The title refers to a running joke between my sister Mildred and me.

I remember Ma straightening Mildred's hair in the kitchen. She seemed to have a very content look on her face whenever she did it. A very different expression from the one she wore whenever she dealt with me.

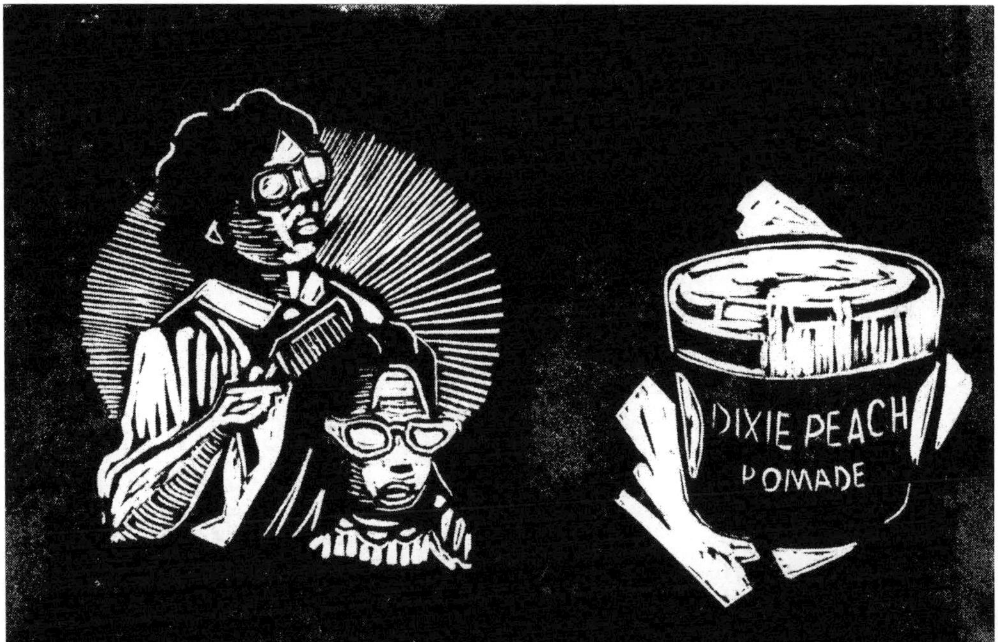
DIXIE PEACH
POMADE

If I Get To Heaven

linocut, 12x12

I remember my three daughters playing in their grandmother's hair. We frequently visited her. Carla and Vicki, and later Val would comb her hair for hours. Ma sat quietly while they did. The girls displayed the same spirit Ma used to show when she cared for Mildred's hair. The title refers to a line in Bill Wither's song *Grandma's Hands*. "If I get to heaven I will look for Grandma's hands." If my girls get to heaven I suppose they would have to look for Grandma’s hair.

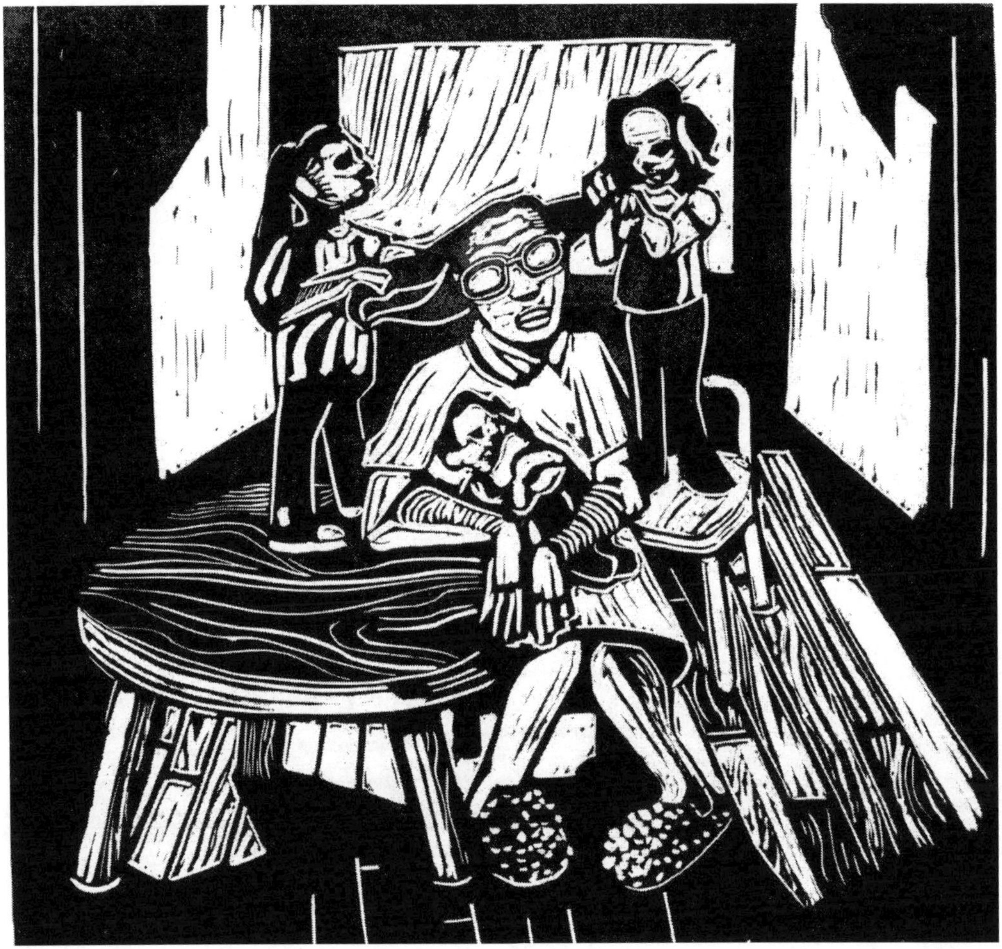

Mindful

linocut, 9x12

My mother was always reading. She loved magazines. Her favorites were *Family Circle, Woman's Day, Reader's Digest*, and *Jet*. She also read books, everything from *Profiles in Courage* to *The Fire Next Time*. Her taste in literature was diverse.

When I was very young we had what seemed like a huge bookcase in our dining room. It was filled to capacity. I realize now it was just an ordinary sized bookcase, but to me it held the world. Our set of encyclopedias introduced me to Pablo Picasso and Vincent Van Gogh. My parents pinched pennies to get the money to pay for that set of books because they believed every family should have a set. It was the beginning of a proper education.

There's an old joke that goes "We grew up so poor we were po. We couldn't afford the other O and R." My family was that kind of poor; we went without things many families would take for granted. We did not, however, go without books. My mother made sure we had plenty to read. Never once did she tell me no when I asked for something to read. She didn't even deny me comic books.

I'm an avid reader also. I inherited that from her. For that I'm eternally grateful.

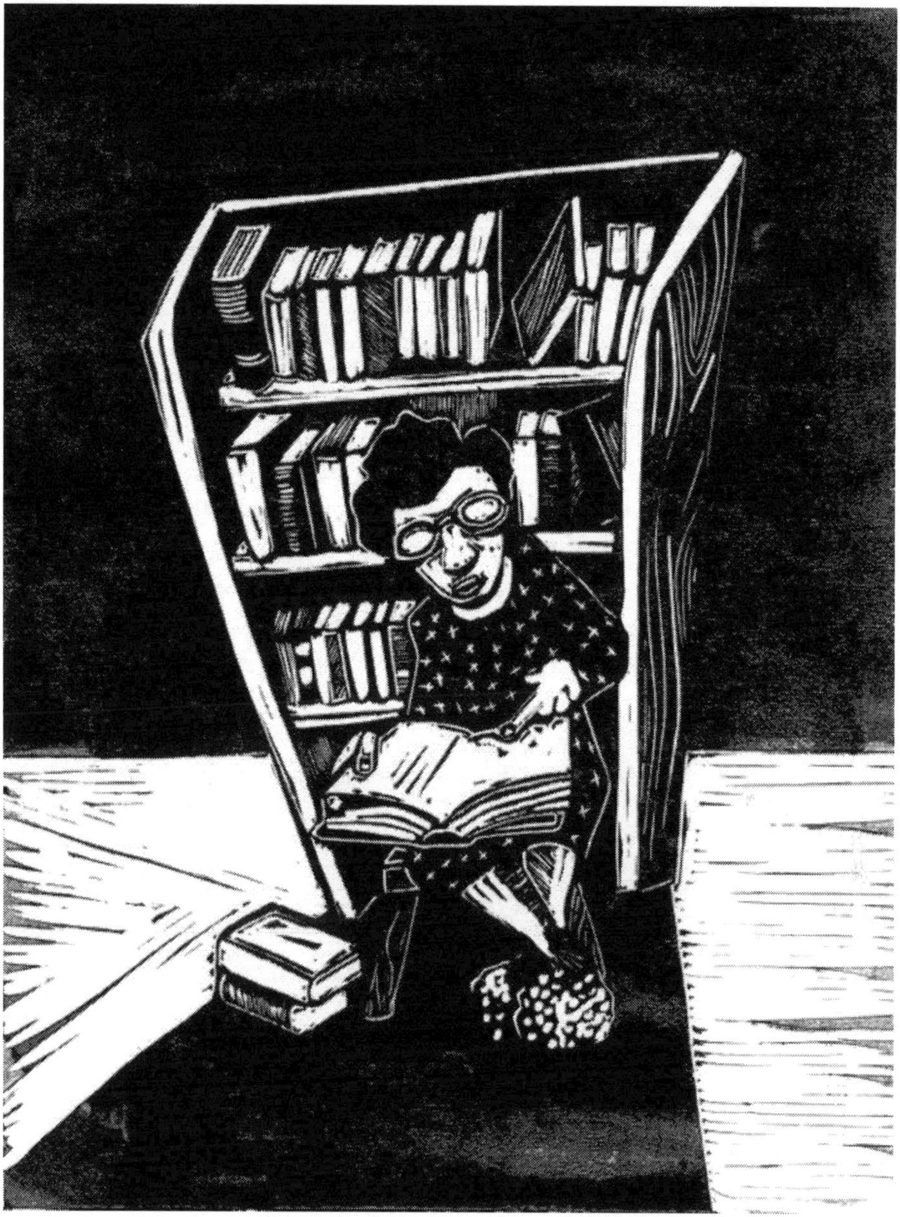

The Good Son

linocut, 9x12

My brother Steven is the most selfless person I know. I could never repay him for the way he has always been there for me and more importantly for Ma. He dutifully waited on her hand and foot for all of his adult life. He never complained. He put his own life on hold to look after her, feed her, and nurse her in times of sickness. He is for a certainty The Good Son.

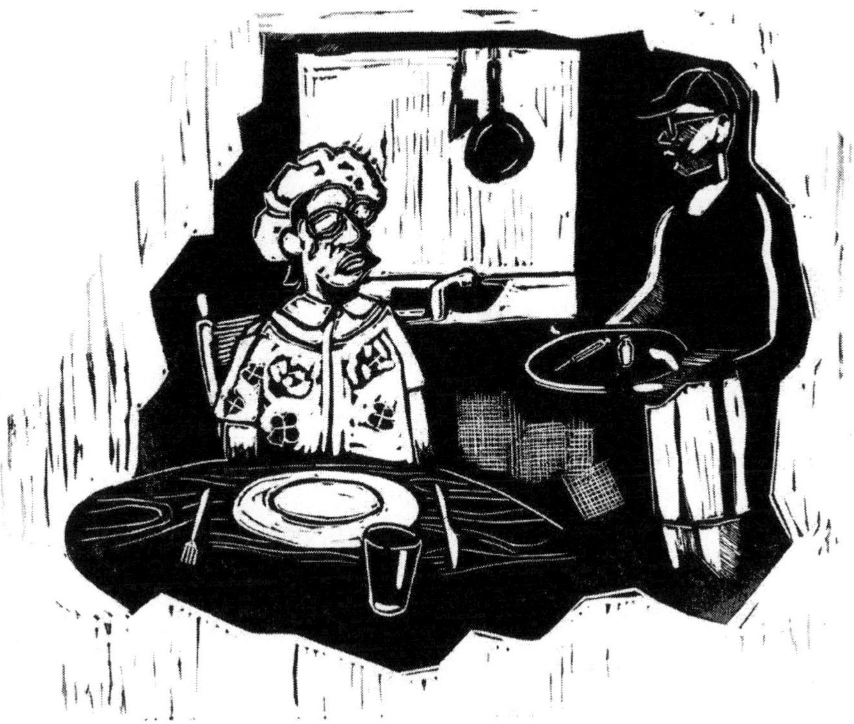

Giant Killer

linocut, 9x12

I had to be one of the dumbest kids on the face of the earth. I was also one of the most troubled kids on earth. I was abused by a weirdo, perverted teacher who got his kicks beating children. You didn't hear much about abuse in those days. My mother figured out something was happening with me, put two and two together and went to the school and confronted this bully of a teacher. He said nothing as Ma read him the riot act. I got dirty looks from him for the rest of the time I was there, but he never once laid his hands on me again. Three times the size of Louise and he fell like a mighty oak. My mother was Louise Wilson, Giant Killer.

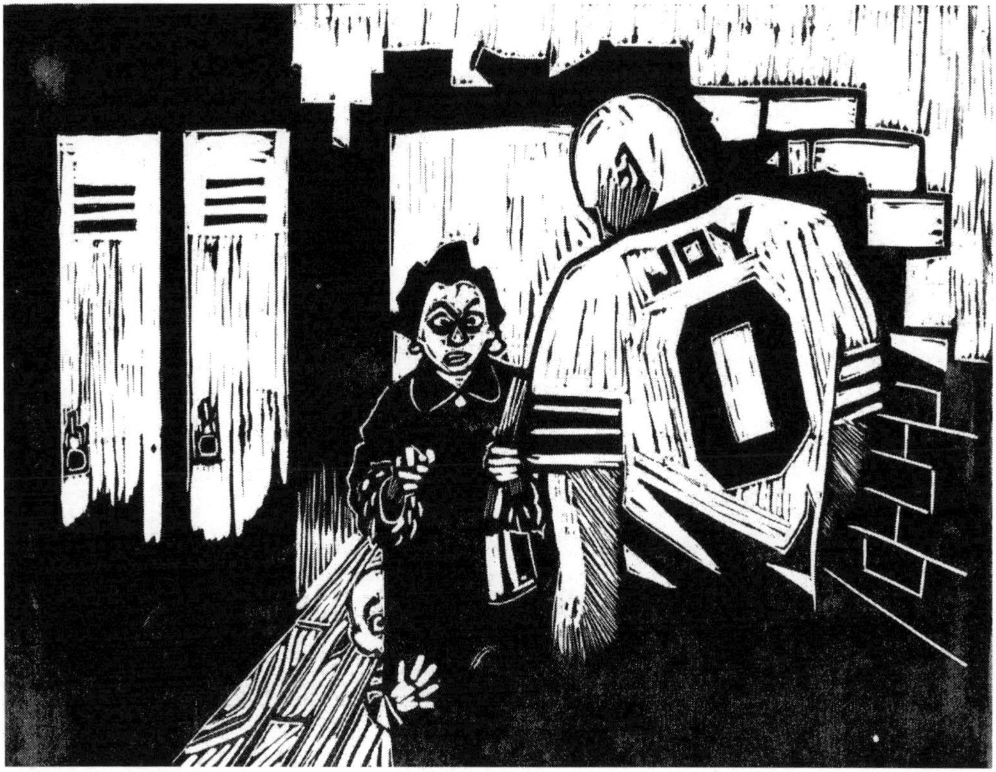

Boy, You Need Jesus

linocut, 9x12

Two hundred years ago when I was a boy, it was a different time. Nurses wore crisp white uniforms, regulation shoes, and special strange hats that had little or nothing to do with handing out pills or sticking people with needles. It was an admirable profession. Black women went to church dressed like nurses and brought glasses of water to folks overcome with the Holy Spirit.

Ma loved church. I hated church. Every minute of it. I thought it was phony and calculated. I could predict what the preacher would say before he said it. That was no amazing feat because the preacher said the same thing every week. What I hated most of all was that church prevented me from watching *The Three Stooges* on Sunday morning.

Ma wasn't having it. None of it. Like a big dummy I got in trouble every Sunday morning for trying to stay home to watch the Stooges. Every Sunday morning I came dangerously close to experiencing her full wrath.

Completely frustrated with me, one Sunday she said I could stay home. I did. I watched the Stooges and laughed not once. I was plagued with guilt. I never tried to stay home again. Thus was the beginning of my warm relationship with God. I learned early what God really wants is for us to love him and feel bad...and not watch Curly.

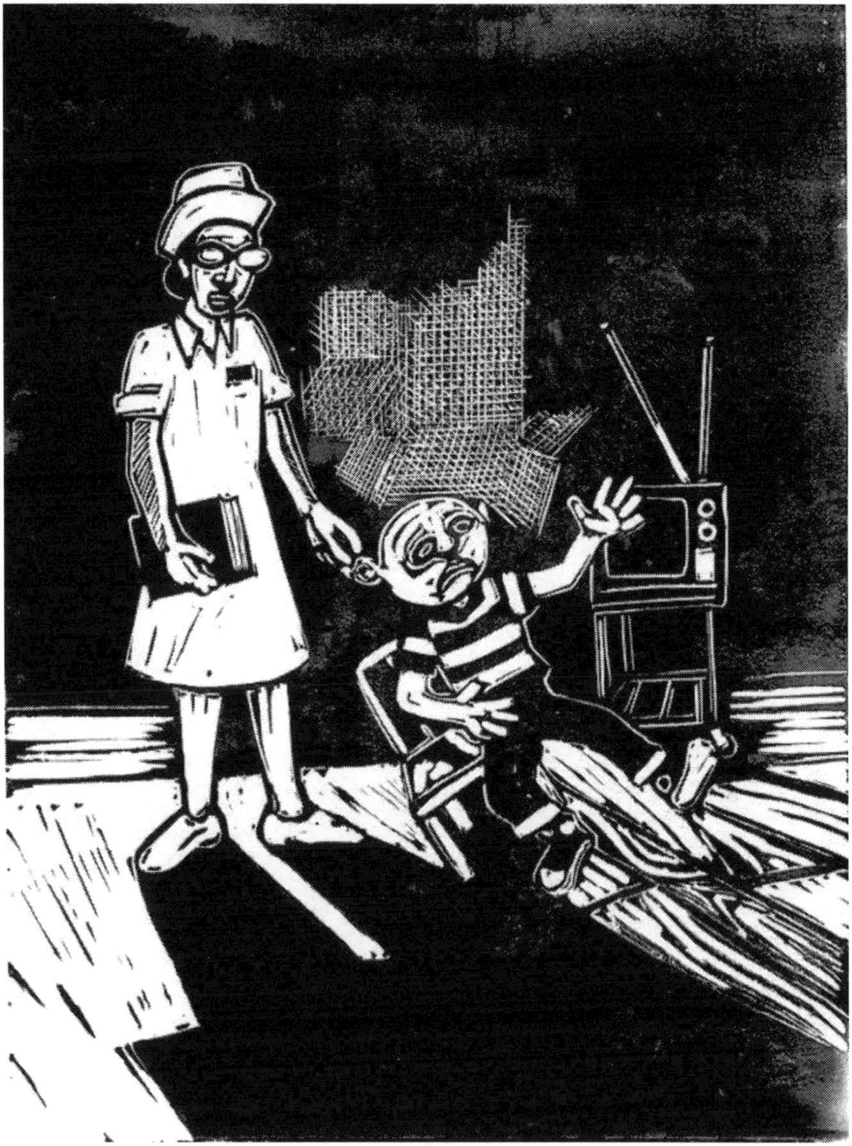

Goodbye

linocut, 9x12

On the evening of June 6, 2003, my sister-in-law called to tell me my mother had a massive heart attack. She had been rushed to the hospital and I needed to get there immediately, as the doctors did not expect her to survive. I was stunned. I was heartbroken, but I did not cry. I arrived to find two of my siblings had made it there before me. Finally, my youngest brother arrived. We took turns speaking our final words to her. I was last. I did something I had never done before. I held her in my arms and said, "I love you Ma." She responded, "I love you too Son," and died in my arms. Neither of us had ever said it before. I wish I had. I'm not ashamed to say I cried when I made this print.

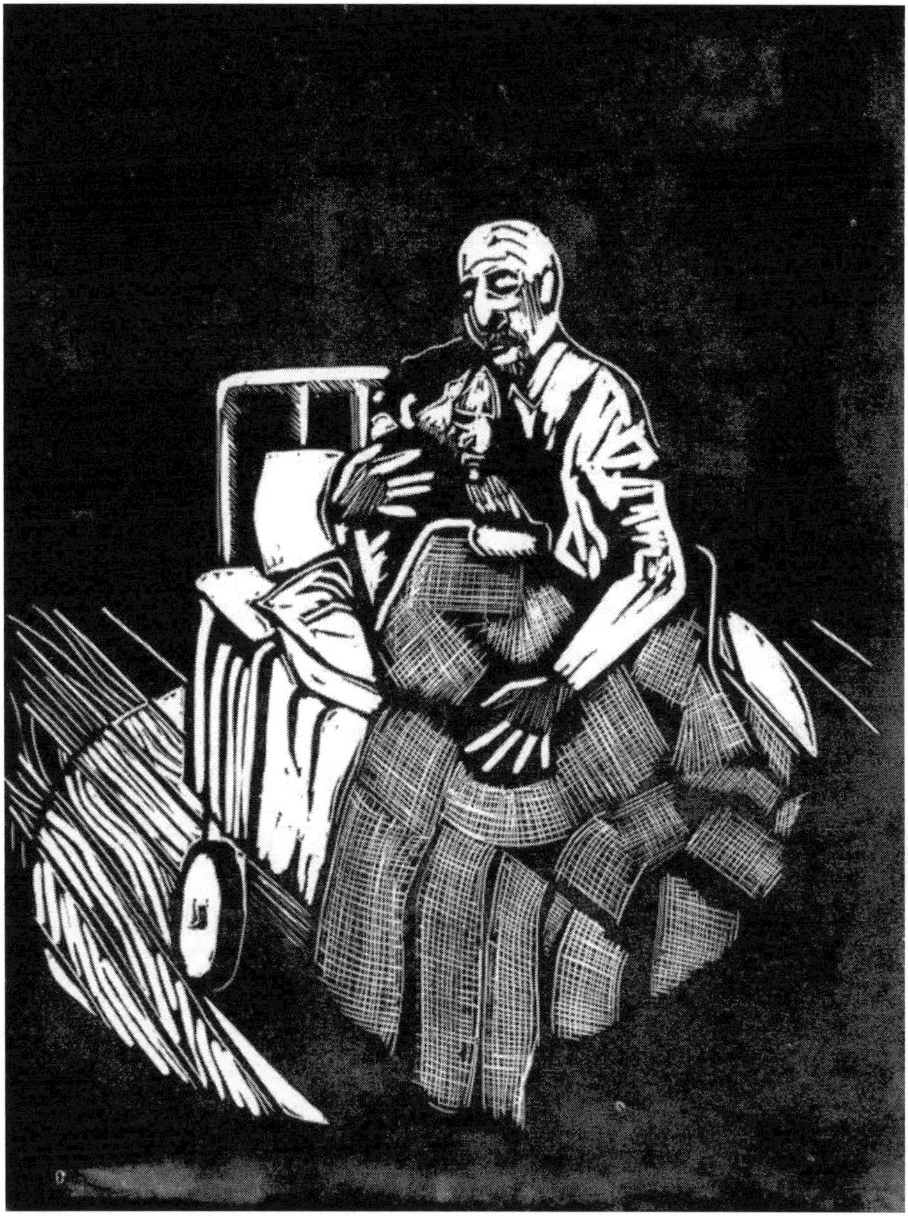

About the Artist

Carl Wilson was born in Detroit, Michigan and currently lives and works in Hamtramck, Michigan. He is a full-time artist specializing in printmaking. Wilson cites surrealist painters and German expressionist printmakers as influences. He deftly sculpts tales of family, friends and the neighborhoods of Detroit onto blocks, creating depictions that are crisp, candid and soulful. His work has been shown in local, national and international exhibitions. In 2013 he received a Kresge Artist Fellowship awarded by Kresge Arts in Detroit, a program of The Kresge Foundation. In addition to enriching his career with a stint as an art curator at a Downtown Detroit gallery and working to publish a periodical featuring Detroit artists, in 2014 he completed a residency at Yaddo in Saratoga Springs, New York.

For more information, visit the artist's website at www.carlwilsonart.com.

33371288R00024

Made in the USA
Lexington, KY
11 March 2019